*30+ Amazing Mindset Tricks &
100+ Daily Affirmations!
Develop a Successful Mindset and
Gain More Self Esteem,
Happiness, Wealth and Freedom
in Your Life! (Successful Mindset,
Mindset for Learning, Growth
Mindset, Millionaire Mindset)*

Kevin Gise © 2015

Disclaimer:

Table of Contents

Introduction

First off, I want to congratulate you on purchasing my book "Mindset: 30+ Amazing Mindset Tricks & 100+ Daily Affirmations! Develop a Successful Mindset and Gain More Self Esteem, Happiness, Wealth, and Freedom in Your Life! (Successful Mindset, Mindset for Learning, Growth Mindset, Millionaire Mindset)". By getting this book you've taken an important first step by investing in your personal growth. Learning how to achieve a proper mindset has the power to completely transform your life in a positive manner.

I've often heard the term "what you think, you will become". I find this rings true when thinking in terms of mindset. The term mindset can be defined as an established set of beliefs and attitudes a person has. If you hold more positive feelings and thoughts about developing skills and improving what you're able to do, you'll end up eventually growing your skill sets and improving yourself. That being said, if you have negative feelings and thoughts, then a lot of the bad things you find happening in your life will continue to occur going forward. By having a negative outlook you're effectively stunting your personal growth and limiting your future opportunities.

There are two main kinds of mindsets a person may have. The first, is a fixed mindset. This is a type of mindset where you're under the belief that your talents and abilities are already set and cannot be meaningfully improved. The second, is a growth mindset. This is a type of mindset where you believe that you can always continue to develop and improve your talents and abilities. Before beginning, you should ask yourself which mindset you associate with.

No matter your age, it's not too late to build the life you want to have. How is it possible to create this new life? Well, you need to begin by adjusting your priorities. Adjusting your priorities will involve having a growth mindset, and squarely focusing on what things matter, and will help you in achieving the life you want to lead. Anything that doesn't help you achieve those goals needs to be set aside.

This book will help walk you through the steps you'll need to take in order to do this. Having a proper mindset is a powerful thing. I hope you get as much out of this process as I did when I first began my own personal journey a few years back.

Let's get started!

Chapter One: Changing Your Mindset Towards Yourself

In this chapter, you will learn:

- Changing Your Mindset Towards Yourself

Changing Your Mindset Towards Yourself

You can't change everything around you without first successfully changing yourself. This section will teach you different techniques to help you transform your mindset and begin making positive changes in your life.

Change isn't immediate. For that reason it's important to learn self discipline and patience. Once you've mastered those skills, you need to learn how to believe in yourself. Only by understanding you hold an unlimited amount of potential, will you be able to move past any fears your still holding onto. and begin to form a clearer picture of what you truly want out of life.

Believing In Yourself

If you're not able to believe in your abilities than who will. It's important to be confident in yourself and your abilities. The first step you need to take to change up your mindset is to begin believing in yourself. Once you've begun to believe in yourself you'll notice that you look to engage more with the world around you. You'll also notice yourself searching out new opportunities and challenges. Instead of feeling down and having a negative fixed mindset you'll have a much more productive positive outlook.

Here are some steps you can take to improve your self belief:

1. Get a journal and write down all the things you love about yourself. Some examples can be your intelligence, you're way with people, sense of humor, and athletic ability. Whatever qualities you pride yourself on having should be written down in this journal.

2. Staying with your journal, you should next write down any skills you possess and any accomplishments you've achieved. You should also write how those skills helped you in the pursuit of your accomplishment. For instance one skill I possess is woodworking. Over the years I've honed my abilities and eventually I used this skill to build a back deck on my parents home as a gift to them. It was my first major project and I felt very accomplished once I had completed it.

3. Next take all your accomplishments and put them into chronological order. How many of those are recent? How many are from longer than 5 years ago? When I first started my journey to changing my mindset I found that my accomplishments had been steadily declining over the last few years. In fact, the more my negative mindset grew the less I began to accomplish.

Once you've gotten all of this written down, you can use it as motivation when you're having negative thoughts. You'll easily be able to reference this and see everything you're good at and all the things you've been able to accomplish in your life. As you begin to accomplish new things and learn new skills add them to your journal. Over time you'll begin to see how much impact having a growth mindset can have on your life.

Facing Your Fears

Your fears won't just disappear on their own. In order to conquer fear you first must face it. When you're trying to grow and accomplish new things you need to be willing to try things you might find scary. In order to get what you want out of life sometimes you'll need to take risks and face a level of uncertainty.

Whether it's asking out that special someone and being afraid of rejection, or leaving a comfortable job and starting your own business in the hopes of something more rewarding, there are times in life where you'll need to overcome your fears and doubts in order to get what you desire.

Facing your fears allows you to expand your mind and grow as a person. When you're no longer afraid of something you're free to pursue it and take advantage of the opportunities it might present. Most of my regrets come from when I let fear control my actions and decisions. When I've faced a fear and still faced rejection or failure I never regretted it because I knew that I took my shot. I understand not everything will work out and I won't always get my way.

Here are some steps you can take to face your fears:

1. Write down your fears and what makes you afraid of it. Knowing exactly what you fear and why you fear it will allow you to understand it and give you insight on how to go about conquering it. Be sure whenever you do overcome something on your list that you cross it out. This will allow you to see the progress you're making, boosting your confidence levels when tackling your other fears.

2. Realize that you're not the only one who is afraid of things. Fear is universal. Don't get worked up or think less of yourself because something scares you. Being afraid is natural. It's not the fear itself, but how you handle the fear that will determine the person you'll end up becoming.

3. Make a separate list of any irrational fears you may be suffering from. What is that you might ask? Well, an irrational fear is a fear that is attached to a specific thing like being afraid to fly, being afraid of clowns, or being afraid of heights.

After you've made your list then make another list of small tasks you can engage in to help you overcome those fears. For instance, if you're afraid of heights start small and go to the top of a small building and look out over the rooftop. Once you've conquered that do the same thing in a bigger building. Eventually you can work you're way up to a level where you're no longer held back by your fear.

One of my friends used to be deathly afraid of heights when she was younger. Eventually she overcame that fear and now she has gone sky jumping on multiple occasions, always raving about what a life changing experience it is. By embracing and overcoming her fear she found something she loves and is passionate about.

4. Remember your previous successes. Think of something you were able to overcome of in the past, using it as motivation to help propel you past the fear you're dealing with currently. I've found this technique really helped me out whenever I hit a roadblock.

5. Always live in the here and now when confronting a fear. Don't let thoughts of the future get you rattled. Just continue to push forward, don't stop until you've overcome the thing you're afraid of.

Determining Purpose

What drives you? What's your idea of happiness? Think about these things and really start to get an idea of what motivates you in life. Maybe you're looking to start a family. Perhaps you're looking to become more successful in business.

Whatever it is that you're looking to accomplish you need to first determine what that is, before you can make any meaningful progress towards your goal of achieving it.

Here are some steps you can take to determine your purpose:

1. Write down what you're passionate about. Make a list of things you'd like to accomplish and what things bring you happiness. These thoughts are meant for only you to look over, so always be completely honest when writing in your journal. Don't add something to your list just because it's something you're expected to want out of life.

2. Discuss all the places and people you care about and love. This will give you greater insight into where your heart truly lies, allowing you to gain a better understanding of what you want and where you want to be. Write down what you'd do if you had nothing limiting you. This will allow you to uncover the things you're most passionate about in life.

3. Take a harder look at all your interests. What are your hobbies? What kind of things do you enjoy in your downtime. Write down all these things and what you enjoy about them. Also write down about the people you care about and what you admire about them. You should also include any role models you may have, and what qualities they possess that inspire you to look up to them. When you learn the qualities you admire most in others, you can begin to model your own behavior to exhibit those same traits and grow as a person.

4. Make a plan of your life in reverse. Start out at what you're life looks like when you're old and retired, working you're way back to the present. This is a great exercise that will allow you to get a glimpse of what you want for your life and then you can work backwards to see what steps you'll need to get there one day.

By finishing all these tasks you'll have a much better understanding of yourself, what you value in others, and what you want out of your life. Learning these things will allow to formulate your goals and begin working towards them.

The Power of Patience

There's a time and place for everything. All your dreams and goals won't be realized overnight. You need to learn how to cultivate patience when it comes to achieving your goals. Timing is often the key to success. Patience gives you the ability to find burgeoning opportunities and will allow you to enjoy living in the moment with what you have currently.

Here are some steps you can take to cultivate patience:

1. Patience will change your perception not only of yourself but of others as well. Having patience allows you to give people the time and creative space to accomplish the tasks you set forth for them. When you're too demanding and impatient with those around you, the results will often suffer because you're not putting them in the best position to succeed. The same can be said for yourself. Being patient allows you to develop as a person and make decisions based on what you want long term, instead of doing something because it provides some temporary instant gratification.

2. Patience allows you to find more opportunity. When you exhibit patience you're able to avoid jumping at the first thing to come your way that only partially fulfills your wants and needs. Instead, you're able to wait on the opportunity that will benefit you the most. For example, maybe you wanted to buy a home but it was currently a seller's market, and due to prices you'd have to settle for less than what you wanted. If you're able to be patient you could wait until the market turns in your favor and get the house you wanted at the same price or even better.

3. Waiting makes people happier. It's been proven scientifically that the longer you're forced to wait for something the more you value it. Instant gratification is great for the short time it lasts. Waiting for what you want will only make you value it more long term.

Success and happiness comes to people who are fluid and accommodating. If you're too rigid and impatient you'll find the road to getting the things you want out of life is much more difficult. Patience allows you to grow as a person and it allows you to set reasonable expectations for the people around you.

Focus

Learning to develop focus will give you the ability to accomplish more and thereby achieve more. Being focused on the things you want in life will help to make you a much happier person. By putting aside things that aren't important to you, all of your attention is squarely focused on things that will benefit you in a positive manner. Reducing your distractions is not always a simple thing. However, if you learn to do so it will allow you to accomplish more than you'd ever thought might be possible.

Here are some steps you can take to develop your focus:

1. Having a morning ritual that includes daily meditation can work wonders. Sit silently for a few minutes every day in a position that's comfortable and work on relaxing and only focusing on your breathing. Push any thoughts aside as they come up. You want to gradually work you're way up to doing this for about 15-20 minutes a day. Once you've finished meditating take a few moments to regain your senses before getting up and continuing your day. Meditation has been shown to improve your clarity and focus throughout the day if you make it into part of your daily routine.

2. Pick one thing and concentrate on it. I like to follow the Pomodoro technique. This basically breaks down your work into 25 minutes intervals timed by a timer followed by short breaks in between. I find this helps to keep me on task and allows me short breaks to let me relax for a few minutes. The belief behind this system is that frequent short breaks will improve your concentration and mental agility. Feel free to to do whatever works for you. The important thing is that you pick a task and work on it, without letting yourself get sucked into different things.

3. Plan out your day in advance. Before I go to bed each evening I make a list of everything I need to accomplish the next day. I find this helps me not only stay organized but helps me to remember important tasks that I might otherwise forget. Personally I use Google Keep to keep me organized. It's free and simple to use, plus it syncs right up to the app on my phone so I can take my list with me wherever I need to go. There are many good web based organizers available I suggest trying some out and seeing which one you like.

Having A Dream

You should have an ultimate goal in life. Something where restrictions and limitations don't matter. This should be something that can only be achieved after a prolonged period of time and will bring significant meaning and happiness to your life. It's important to always have something to strive for. It will keep you motivated when times are tough and will stop you from becoming complacent as your smaller goals are met.

1. Write down your dreams in detail. You need to get specific. You can always modify, add or change your dream as you continue to grow and learn more about yourself but you initially want to have a strong idea of what your dream entails so you can go about working to achieve it.

2. You need to have some desire to accomplish your dreams. If you're not motivated towards achieving your dream than maybe you're dream isn't your dream after all. You need to find something that drives you and gives you a reason to move forward and grow as an individual. You should always ask yourself if what you're doing is getting you closer to reaching your dream, or is it actually putting it further out of reach. When you find things are taking you away from accomplishing your dreams you need to find ways to focus on only what's important.

3. Take massive action! Always be moving forward and trying to make headway. While I do preach patience when it better serves your long term needs, there's always something else going on in your life that you can be taking action on in order to work towards your goals. Know what you're goals are and how you want to get there. It will make any actions you take more efficient. I also always review the action I've taken to see where I could improve my time management going forward.

4. Don't be afraid of failure. No one is successful all the time. Everyone will fail. The important part is to learn from your failures and continue pushing forward. A famous example of this is Abraham Lincoln. During the course of his life he failed in business, had his sweetheart die, had a nervous breakdown, failed when running for office on at least 4 different occasions and yet still he persevered and eventually won the presidency.

My advice is to enjoy yourself during the process and don't let your happiness be dictated by the outcome. If things don't go your way pick up yourself up and find a new way to remove any of the hurdles that may be blocking your path. Remember the more you believe in yourself the more your positive your mindset will become naturally over time. Don't let negative beliefs or a negative outcome stand in your way.

Chapter Two: Changing Your Mindset Towards Others

In this chapter, you will learn:

- Changing Your Mindset Towards Others

Changing Your Mindset Towards Others

This section will go over the importance of changing your mindset towards the other people in your life. This includes family members, friends, business contacts and anyone else you come into contact with. You'll learn some tips and methods on how to better treat and appreciate the people around you.

You'll also learn the importance of always being surrounded by "good company" and how who you're surrounded by often dictates your level of success and happiness. This section will go over connecting with new people and forming more friendships. I'll also discuss how by helping other people achieve there goals it will help you achieve yours as well.

Keep Good Company

When trying to change your mindset and better your life, you should actively try and surround yourself with positive people who encourage and inspire you to reach for your dreams. It's been shown that people are influenced tremendously by the people they keep company with. If you're friends are negative and have a "can't do" attitude it's more than likely that you're going to have a more negative mindset than someone surrounded by people who are positive and supportive.

There's exceptions to every rule but why chance it. When you find yourself meeting new people who are fun and encouraging you should try and make an effort to befriend them and use their positive energy as inspiration.

Here are some steps you can take to keep good company and improve the relationships you already have:

1. Forgive mistakes and wrongs done against you. Don't let yourself get caught up in negative energy. The easier you're able to forgive those around you when they hurt you, the more you'll be able to find people who will be supportive and positive. You also need to learn how to forgive yourself. Being negative towards yourself will hinder your ability to embrace a new growth mindset.

2. Be aware of what you're thinking and feeling. Showing others the same respect and love you want for yourself will bring a better group of people into your circle of friends, improving your current relationships. Give happiness to receive happiness is something I truly believe in. Remember people come from all different types of backgrounds and mindsets. Try and put yourself in there shoes before you get upset with them over something you consider to be rude or insensitive. Just because they don't think the same way as you doesn't mean they aren't worth your respect and kindness.

Meet New People

Every day brings us an opportunity to meet and learn from new people. Life is about the connections we make with others. If you're shy try to step a little bit out of your comfort zone by trying to turn a stranger into a friend. I was very shy when I was first starting out so this was one of the hurdles I had to overcome. Now I'm constantly meeting new people and building new relationships. I find it to be extremely rewarding, and at times beneficial to my overall goals.

Here are some steps you can take to meet new people:

1. Realize that most people are generally friendly. Making new friends and meeting new people doesn't need to feel scary. The more you get out there and engage with people the easier it will get to continue doing so. Go into meeting others with a positive attitude, strike up a conversation, listen when they talk, and hope for the best. All you need to do is go up and introduce yourself.

2. Don't be afraid to put yourself out there. Like I mentioned before I was once shy so putting myself out there made me feel uncomfortable. That being said after I did it a few times it became easier and easier to do. Now I feel uncomfortable if I'm around others and not trying to interact with them. I've met some of my best friends this way, as well as a few great business contacts. Rejection will happen. Don't let it get you down or take it personally! Not everyone will have the same mindset as you do.

Don't Be Judgmental

You don't like it when others unfairly judge you, so why would you continue doing it to those you meet and interact with. This can be a tough one for many people as judging others is often ingrained into they way we deal with others from a young age. We see others do it in movies, music and real life all the time so we begin to do it ourselves until it becomes like second nature to us.

This type of thinking will keep you stuck in a fixed mindset. There's not only one way to do things and view the world. Everyone has their own thoughts and opinions. It's not our place to say they're incorrect and judge them for not thinking along the same lines as we do. When you're able to stop judging those around you, it allows you to build stronger and healthier relationships with them.

This is how I try and work through things to become less judgmental:

Identify what and who you're judging. Is it something about yourself, someone else, an activity, a situation or a place. Once you've figured out what is bothering you, take a moment to reflect on specifically what is causing you to have a negative response.

After you've determined the what and the why, it's time to find a way to see past the thing causing you to act judgmental. Fill your mind with positive thoughts and try to keep an open mind and open heart.

If you're dealing with a person, or a situation caused by those around you, try and put yourself into the other people's shoes and see what might be causing them to act the way they are acting.

If you're dealing with a place or an activity that's bringing up a negative response, try and find something positive about it. Understand just because it's not something or somewhere you enjoy, doesn't mean it's not something others won't. Always remember everyone is unique.

We all have our own likes, dislikes, quirks and views on how we see the world. There's value to everyone and everything. If you take the time to see it instead of being judgmental from the get go you'll open up a world of new opportunities and relationships you'd otherwise would have closed yourself off from.

Enjoy The Process

Life is a journey. You need to enjoy the ride and not just the results. If you're not taking any joy from your life while chasing your dreams then you're making a serious mistake in your approach to life. The journey is what helps to build your character as a person. You won't always succeed but even your failures will offer valuable lessons.

When you focus on the process, you're building good habits, which will benefit you down the road. Enjoying yourself during the journey will allow you to push harder and achieve more. It will also help to build your confidence and give you the right attitude to work past obstacles as they come at you.

Not enjoying yourself will lead to you getting burned out before you're able to achieve your goals. Happiness will make you more dedicated and will also make you more willing to get back up when you get knocked down.

Enjoying the process will also give you the patience necessary to get where you want to go. There's a famous saying "Rome wasn't built in a day". What this means is that it takes time to build the life you want. Things won't all happen overnight. I'd rather live a life of happiness and see some of my goals go unfulfilled rather than live a joyless life for years at a time, but eventually reach my goals.

Help Others Succeed

I once heard the quickest way to reach your own goals was to always be helping other people reach their goals. Helping other people will open up your world in ways you can't imagine. It can be one of the most rewarding personal experiences you'll ever have.

Over the years I've made many new friends and business contacts by giving value and helping others get to where they wanted to go in life. Not only does it help to nourish your soul, but it teaches you a lot about life and the power of people helping each other.

Here are some steps you can take to help others succeed:

1. Volunteer your time. This can feel difficult when you're juggling a lot of your own things that need to get done. However, trust me when I say it's well worth the time. Carving out a little bit of time from your schedule is easy to do if you're willing to make an effort. You can volunteer for a few hours a week or a few hours a month, it doesn't need to take up a big part of your life. Personally, I worked my way up from a few hours a month to about 5 hours a week.

2. Make introductions. Once you've been at this for a while you'll begin to build up a pretty sizable list of contacts. Now if someone I know is trying to do something, or trying to fix a problem, I can often put them in contact with someone I know that can help them in their situation. This doesn't take up much of my time, and it can make a real difference.

3. Offer your feedback. If you have something to offer that you find constructive and helpful be sure to let your friends or business partners know about it. Some people don't take kindly to feedback, but that's them usually being negative and judgmental. You should always make the offer, if they don't accept it then at least you tried to help.

Chapter Three: How To Become A Better Version Of Yourself

In this chapter, you will learn:

- How To Become A Better Version Of Yourself

How To Become A Better Version Of Yourself

In this section I'm going to discuss what steps you should be taking in order to become the best version of yourself. This is something you'll be working on your entire life. There's always room for improvement. No one will ever be perfect but it is something to strive towards.

Challenge Yourself and Take Risks

Many of us avoid doing things we deem challenging or risky. At times these things feel too difficult, and impossible to succeed at. People will often choose being comfortable over being happy. The reason for this is because they have a fixed mindset, and don't believe they'll be able to accomplish the goals that will lead to eventual happiness.

Many people, myself included, have only looked at what can go wrong in a situation, thinking that failure is inevitable. This type of negative thinking has you magnifying the probability of failure until you've convinced yourself not even to give it a try. This leads to people sticking to their normal routines and never venturing out and taking risks.

Things won't change in your life unless you're a catalyst for change. You need to be continually stepping out of your comfort zone and pushing your boundaries. It's the only way to significantly grow as a person, and it will give you the growth mindset needed to meet any challenges that come your way.

Here are some steps you can take:

1. Believe that you will succeed at whatever you try and accomplish.

2. Plan out your goals and how you will reach them.

3. Take massive action on your plan

4. Constantly evaluate the results of any actions you've taken

5. Move on to the next goal and repeat the process.

When you break things down they feel much easier to accomplish. I like to break all my goals down into smaller steps. I know that by focusing on one small step at a time I can eventually get to where I want to go. It also helps to keep me motivated and on track because I'm constantly completing tasks, keeping my forward momentum going.

Be Discerning

The world is filled with distractions. From websites, smart phones, and television alone, people will often lose hours of each day. Being able to put down those distractions, focusing all your energy on important tasks, will make it much easier for you to start seeing positive changes in your life.

I would take a day and spend it as you normally would. The only difference is I want you to keep a log of everything you're doing and how you long you were doing it for. Try and be as honest as possible. This list is only for you. At the end of the day see how much time was lost due to distractions and fluff. Also calculate how much time was spent working towards your goals and dreams.

Most of you will find that you're spending way more time on distractions then you had previously thought. You'll also find that you weren't devoting nearly enough time to productive tasks. What I suggest is taking the amount of time you spent being distracted and organize some productive tasks you could accomplish using that time going forward.

I have both an overall plan on things I want to accomplish and a daily plan on what I want to get done each day. Cut out all distractions for a few days and work on things that you deem to be important. At the end of those few days evaluate your progress and see how much more you're were able to get done when you remained focused.

After a few days are over, you can add some time back in for a little distraction. Everyone needs downtime to recharge. I just want you to try and see what a difference being completely focused on your goals can make in a short amount of time. I also want you to realize that you might be wasting more time than you initially thought you were each day. Even cutting back on your distractions a little can make a huge difference over the course of a few months or years.

Failure is Gift

While failure often stings, and can get us feeling down, remember it is often our greatest teacher. Failure is the thing that helps us grow the most as a person. Many people will look at failure from a fixed mindset, using it as way to show that they weren't meant to do something or succeed. You need to view it from a growth mindset, realizing that every failure is a just another step towards eventual success.

I know that anytime I've ever failed at something I've learned an incredible amount from it. I take the time to look at each failure and break down the things I did right and the things I did wrong. Learning what not to do is often just as important as learning what to do.

Here's a stat you may not know. About half of all business will fail in their first 3 years. That's a crazy sounding number but it's true. However, you're only ever truly a failure if you don't get back up and begin trying again. Inaction is the only true form of failure.

Here are some steps you can take to succeed:

1. Learn what being successful will require in whatever you're trying to be successful at.

2. Make a list of all your strengths and weaknesses that pertain to what you're trying to accomplish. I'd then advise having some of the people you trust assess you, and give you feedback to see if you're ideas of yourself meet up with how your viewed by those close to you.

I find that many of us will often get a few of our own strengths and weaknesses wrong at times. Getting the perspective of others will give you a clearer picture of yourself.

3. Always be looking to improve your weaknesses and build on your strengths. Don't be afraid to get the help of others in areas you need help. Your goals don't care who helped you accomplish them. Don't let your ego get in the way of your success.

4. Always plan ahead. Know where you're at and where you want to get to. I always try and plan out where I envision myself in the next month, 6 months and 5 years. I feel like having those check in points will allow me to see how much progress I've made, and whether I'm on track, ahead of schedule, or need to be focusing more time and energy on a particular area of my life.

Try New Things

As you work towards your goals and find success in accomplishing your tasks you'll find that you are often motivated by the progress you make. However, at some point, most of us will hit roadblocks. These can be brought on by different things happening in our life, such as the loss of a loved one, injury, or sickness. Roadblocks can also be brought on by our own self doubt, fear, and negative thinking.

As much as we try, sometimes these negative feelings will find a way to bubble up to the surface and will begin affecting us. In order to combat this we need to constantly be finding new and exciting ways to grow as a person. One of the ways to open our minds and grow is by having new experiences and trying new things.

I know I often get a rush of positive energy after I've gone out and tried something new for the first time. These experiences are nourishment for the soul, invigorating you, and getting you out of whatever funk you're currently experiencing. Feeling down is natural at times but there's nothing that says you shouldn't try and actively shake off that feeling. You should always be striving to get back to being a happier you.

Here are some examples of new experiences you may want to try:

1. Changing up your daily routine to include something new. For example, every few months I take a new class. These classes have ranged from painting to Krav Maga. I enjoy learning new things. Some things like painting I realize I'm not passionate about, so I stop, and others like Krav Maga I really enjoy and continue to practice.

2. Trying new foods. Before I started this journey I had a very boring palette. I had a small group of foods I liked and I stuck only to those foods. Now I'm up for trying anything at least once. I've learned that I enjoy many more types of food than I originally believed.

3. Meeting new people. I went over this one earlier but I really enjoy building new relationships. I find it incredibly invigorating.

4. Mastering a new skill. I recently began woodworking. I was never very hands on when I was growing up but I've found it to be a rewarding experience now that I'm older.

5. Reading and learning. I try and read a new book at least every couple of weeks. I have a list of about 50 books that I want to get through and I'm frequently checking ones off and adding new ones to the list.

6. Visiting new places. I love to travel. It's my favorite thing to do. I find it to be incredibly important to my continued happiness. Hopefully I'll make it to all seven continents at some point. I've made it to four and counting!

On a side note, I always enjoy the experiences above more when I share them with others I'm close to. I suggest doing some of these with your friends and loved ones whenever possible.

Chapter Four: Changing Your Mindset Towards Money

In this chapter, you will learn:

- Changing Your Mindset Towards Money

Changing Your Mindset Towards Money

Each person has there own relationship when it comes to money. If your mindset says that there's never enough money and you want to hold on to it, you may need to change up your mindset. Remember, money is just a means to an end. Money is one of the means we can use to help us reach our goals and dreams. Money shouldn't be the only reason for doing something. When it's the sole reason you'll find the results will never end up satisfying you.

In this section I'm going to discuss how you can work on your relationship with money and how by changing your mindset you can use it to help you reach your dreams.

Do Something You Love

I believe that if you do something you love and are passionate about, then the money will follow. If you aren't passionate about what you're doing it will be much more difficult to become successful at it, and to maintain any success you achieve long term.

It's been proven that people who engage in activities they love will earn a higher salary in those fields. Passion fuels success. The more you care, the more you'll put into the work, and the more you'll get back in return.

Here are some examples of how you can turn what you love into your job:

1. Start off doing it on the side as a hobby. Many of the most successful people in the world first started their business at home, part time, while they worked other jobs. This is a good way to learn the ropes, gain needed experience, and meet new business contacts without having to risk your families future by quitting your current job.

2. Always be improving and learning new things in your field. You should always be trying to push forward and innovate. People who are able to to do this will ultimately find more success than those who just follow behind what others come up with.

3. When you see an opportunity take it. The goal is to turn what you love doing into your work. This means when you find an opportunity to go full time you need to take a risk and try it. I know it can be scary but once you feel you're ready to take your part time job to full time you need to make the leap. Remember, even when you fail you learn and grow as a person.

Be Grateful

You should always be very grateful for all the things you have. Nothing in life is certain or guaranteed. Being thankful for what you have will make you appreciate all the hard work you put in, along with the all the hard work of the others around you. The more you appreciate things, the more you'll value you them, and the harder you'll work to achieve them.

Here are some ways to help yourself remain grateful:

1. Write down what you happen to be grateful about each day. This is a great little exercise I do every morning as part of my morning ritual. It helps remind me of how blessed I am and what good can happen when I work hard and go after my dreams. These lists are also great to have when you're feeling down and need something to lift your spirits.

2. Be mindful. There is a ton of things you can look forward to every day. Being mindful will allow you to improve your overall sense of happiness. I've always found the more positive my mindset the more I'm able to accomplish. Negativity is like an anchor that can make completing even the simplest of activities extremely difficult.

3. Share the things you're appreciative of with others that are close to you. I find this let's others around me know that I care about them by sharing more of my life with them. It also allows me to get other people excited about helping me achieve my goals.

Constantly being grateful has a big effect on your mindset. Soon you'll find yourself having less negative thoughts on a daily basis. This will not only lead to further personal growth, but it will keep you open to new opportunities and new ways to get the money you need to reach your goals.

Carefully Budget

Having a growth mindset is wonderful but you still need to budget accordingly and carefully manage your money. You want every dollar working for you. This means you need to know all your income coming in and expenses going out.

Crafting a budget will not only teach you to value your money it will show you that it's possible to save for the future and set money aside to help you get to where you want to end up in life.

Here are some ways to help you budget:

1. Begin tracking all your income. Make a list of everything you need to spend each month. Then begin tracking all your daily incidentals to get an idea of what you're spending your extra income on. This will let you find things you can cut out or cut back spending on. Most people don't realize how much money they waste each month on trivial things.

2. Create your budget. Once you've got all your income and expenses mapped out it's time to make a monthly budget. Try and stick to this as closely as possible. Always leave a certain amount set aside each month for unforeseen emergencies. Things will happen that aren't in your budget and will cost you money. It's a good idea to have something set aside for when it does.

3. When you blow your budget (and you will early on), be sure to learn from the mistakes and adjust your budget accordingly going forward. You need to be realistic when creating a budget. It's important to be able to follow your budget, so you'll have the ability to save for the things you'll need to reach your goals.

How to Save Money

This is a difficult one for many people. I know when I first started, any money coming in went right back out the door. Saving takes discipline and practice.

Here are some ways to help you learn how to save money:

1. Begin with small goals. I find it best to start small and work your way up when beginning to save. This will allow you to see it's possible and will keep you from getting discouraged by trying to save too much too quickly and failing. I try to increase the amount I save a little each month. Over time it really begins to add up.

2. Minimize expenses. In order to save you'll need to cut back on your spending. Most of us waste money each month on entertainment, going out to eat, and a variety of other things that aren't necessary. When you're making your budget try to cut down on the unnecessary expenses and divert those extra funds towards your savings.

3. Look at your savings as an expense. I like to think of this as my most important expense because it's the money I'm going to use to build my future and fuel all of my dreams. When you begin viewing your savings like this it instills saving money as something that is necessary instead of as something you can do when you have a few extra dollars laying around.

Invest What You Earn

Making your money work for you is an excellent way to grow your wealth. Once you've saved up some money it's time to begin finding ways to invest. Always remember to leave enough in savings to cover any types of emergencies that may arise.

I suggest starting slow, diversifying, and get used to investing before diving in full bore. The reason I say this is because like any new endeavor you're bound to make a mistake or two. I'd hate for those rookie mistakes to cost you a chunk of the money you had been saving.

Personally I like investing in mutual funds. I'm able to pick a group of companies I like and once I invest I have a nice portfolio of different stocks. When I first started out I did a lot of research on different online brokerage accounts and all the pro's and con's associated with investing in mutual funds. Once I felt informed on the subject I applied for the brokerage account I thought fit my needs the best and opened an account.

This is not a book on investing advice so I'm not going to try and tell you what you should invest your money in. I picked mutual funds, but I have friends who do options trading, others that invest in companies that offer micro loans, and friends who invest a variety of other opportunities. It's all about doing your due diligence and putting you're money where you're most comfortable investing.

Chapter Five: 30 Quick Ways to Improve Your Mindset

In this chapter, you will learn:

- 30 Quick Ways to Improve Your Mindset

30 Quick Ways to Improve Your Mindset

Here are 30 quick things you should consider when trying to improve your mindset. Some are actions you can take to better yourself, while others are mantras and things you should reflect on a daily basis.

1. Have a morning ritual. This is a great way to set yourself up for success on a daily basis. Every morning I have a 45 minute ritual I use to help me prepare for the day. My ritual consists of meditation, yoga, personal affirmations, reflection and organizing my day. I find that having this time in the morning helps me get focused and ready for the day ahead. Everyone's ritual may be different but having one will make a big difference.

2. Take the time to take care of yourself. You're nothing without your health. You should take pride in not only your health but also your appearance. Taking time away from your family and business can feel selfish at times but you need to carve at some time to work on yourself. I have a daily workout routine (except Sunday) and weekly Krav Maga class.

3. Stop comparing yourself to other people. We often fall into the habit of negatively comparing ourselves to those around us. You need to focus on yourself. You don't know everything about the people you're comparing yourself to. Usually you're only taking the positive attributes you see about them and extrapolating that to all facets of their life. You need to learn to believe in yourself and your abilities. You're only wasting your energy by focusing on comparing yourself to others.

4. Don't be held back by past actions. Don't let your past dictate your future. You need to give yourself permission to move on from prior failures and previous action. A growth mindset means you're always striving to improve and better your life and situation.

5. Make a list of how you contribute to making the lives of those around you better. I suggest writing down your best qualities, and how you improve the lives of your friends and loved ones.

6. Don't be held back by failure. There will be times you don't succeed. Perseverance is an important quality to have. Always look at every problem as just another opportunity for you to solve. Failure builds character and leads to personal growth.

7. Everything I need will come to me in due time. Don't feel like you need to reach your goals overnight. That's just not feasible. Patience is it's own reward. Enjoy the journey and don't try to rush success. If you do, you're more prone to making mistakes that will cost you in the long run.

8. Personal affirmations are a great way to keep you motivated and in a positive mindset. I have a list of affirmations I run through on a daily basis during my morning ritual. You should find some affirmations that get you motivated and keep them accessible. I'll discuss mine in the next chapter.

9. Focus on continual improvement. You should be working on bettering yourself a little more each day. You'll always be able to improve some area of you're life. There's no such thing as perfection. Always finding new things to work on will help you grow as a person and keep you motivated long term.

10. Don't get too hard on yourself when thinking about your faults. You need to have a positive loving mindset when you think of yourself. If you're not able to remain positive about yourself, you'll have a difficult time remaining positive towards others. Would you belittle your friends and family members for their flaws or mistakes. Of course you wouldn't! Therefore you shouldn't be doing it to yourself either.

11. Remind yourself that you are a good person who is deserving of happiness and love. Constantly reinforcing the positive attributes about yourself will help to make them a part of yourself going forward. You'll achieve much more with a positive self image. If you can't love yourself and realize the value you offer than how will others.

12. Don't forget to enjoy the journey. Be happy with your current situation. Even though you may be aspiring for greater heights it's okay to enjoy what you have, even when it's not what you want to end up with. You never know the hand life is going to deal you so it's best to appreciate the present while working towards the future.

13. Don't forget that you're capable and smart enough to overcome any of the problems that may pop up along the way. Issues will constantly pop up to challenge you. It's just a fun fact of life. Going into your problems with a positive mindset will allow you to overcome hurdles much more effectively.

14. Follow your dreams no matter the cost. You only get one life. Don't waste it by not going after the things you want out of life. That would be the biggest disservice you could ever do to yourself.

15. Show compassion to yourself and to others around you. Everyone has there reasons for doing the things they do, even if you don't agree with them. Being able to show compassion is a sign of maturity, and will take up much less energy and focus than getting angry and worked up about something.

16. You know what 's best for you and your future. Your life is your own. You need to be the one to make decisions on how you plan on spending it. It's important to remember that you're the main protagonist of your own life. Don't less yourself feel relegated to a secondary character by those around you.

17. Don't hold on to your fear, anger and worries. These things will drain your energy and impede your ability to focus on your objectives. You need to banish these negative thoughts and feelings from your life as best as possible. Whenever I begin to feel down I always try and do things that will lift my spirit and reinvigorate me. This can be as simple as repeating a few affirmations, to taking some time out of my day to do something I enjoy and makes me happy.

18. Be accepting of others, even when they are not what you want them to be. Don't push your expectations onto people. You wouldn't want others to do that to you. By accepting others for who they are, you will be able to form healthier and longer lasting relationships. You also won't be let down when they don't meet some secret expectations you think they should be meeting. The only person that you can change is yourself. Working on yourself will take a lifetime, so don't waste your energy trying to mold others into the person you would like them to be.

19. Today will bring you happiness and joy. Going into each day believing that statement will allow you to get the most out of each experience. Anger is a choice. Don't let negativity ruin your day. It's unproductive and accomplishes nothing in the long run.

20. Believe that you will attract wealth and love in abundance. Having the mindset that you will get the things you want out of life will allow you to take more opportunities when they arise. Most people let a "can't do" attitude stop them from seizing an opportunity in the small window of time it presents itself in. When you remain positive and expect these opportunities to come, you'll be fully prepared to jump at them before they pass you by.

21. You play the deciding role in your own success. The amount of success you achieve is primarily up to you. Occasionally there will be other influences that either help or hinder your progress. However, in the long term the amount of success you have will be dictated primarily by you and what you do to get it.

22. Your thoughts create your reality. There's a famous phrase " I think, therefore I am". What you choose to focus on will have an big impact on your day. That's why by choosing to think positively you'll be more likely to do things that will make your day a better one.

23. Surround yourself with people who value you and respect the things you have to offer. It's often said we end up becoming the people we surround ourselves with. That means if you surround yourself with positive and productive people you'll eventually become productive and positive also. I found that once I cut out the people who were negative influences in my life I became much happier overall and found more success in life. You want the people around you to lift you higher, not tear you down.

24. Building relationships builds the world around you and opens doors to new opportunities. I find the more people I meet and build relationships with, the more I can accomplish. Over the years I've built up a network of friends and business contacts I can go to whenever I need a helping hand or want a second opinion. Not only that, but I've met some of my closest friends and loved ones because I made it a point to become more social and expand my circle.

25. Be willing to forgive yourself and others. Everyone makes mistakes. Don't hold them over their heads or your own. It doesn't add any value to your life and holding on to that type of negative energy will do more harm than good.

26. Your family is a gift. Even though they may drive you crazy at times, you're family is a gift. They will teach you how to deal with conflicting personalities and ideologies. Your family will help you grow as a person and will teach you many valuable lessons throughout your life.

27. Trust your inner voice. Sometimes knowing the right thing to do can be difficult and confusing. If you've done all the research and the path is still unclear you should trust what your instincts are telling you to do.

28. Practice meditation. I find that meditating every day provides a level of clarity you won't normally have. It takes some time to get used to it so be patient. I know once I got the hang of it, I was blown away by how much of a change it made in my life. It helped to keep me focused and in a positive growth mindset.

29. Take time out of your schedule for your friends and loved ones. No matter how busy I get chasing my dreams I always set aside time to spend with the people who are important to me. It's important to have time focused solely on them. It will not only help to keep your relationships in good standing but it will also keep you from getting burned out and worn down.

30. Start today! There's no time like the present. Why hold off what you can start on today until tomorrow. You need to get used to taking action and making moves. The present is all we have so it's best to make the most of it.

Chapter Six: The 100+ Daily Affirmation Cheat Sheet

In this chapter, you will learn:

- The 100+ Daily Affirmation Cheat Sheet

The 100+ Daily Affirmation Cheat Sheet

In this section I'll be giving you a list of the daily affirmations I use every morning during my morning ritual. These affirmations are a constant source of both inspiration and motivation. They help to keep me on the right track even when negative thoughts and feelings start to creep in. Feel free to use whatever affirmations work for you. Everyone is unique, so even though I find these to be helpful, some of you may not feel the same way about some of them. Experiment with different things until you find a system that consistently keeps you in a positive state of mind.

Some people have a hard time believing that affirmations are helpful. Initially I was one of those skeptics. However, a friend convinced me to try it for a month and see how I felt then. I took my friend's advice and was amazed with the results. My affirmations provide both a sense of happiness to my life and help me achieve my goals. Two things I was struggling with beforehand. I'm hopeful that they'll be able to help you out also.

When using your affirmations remember to use them in a present tense. Also repeat them out loud, and with authority if possible. You want to to really commit to these when you're saying them. You want to embrace what you're saying and believe them. The more you begin to do this the more positive your mindset will eventually become.

1. I love myself and I'm worthy of my dreams.

2. I am a gift to the world and deserve love and respect.

3. I am loved by my friends and family.

4. I make the choices for my life.

5. Following my heart and my instinct will keep me on the right path.

6. I take joy even when I'm on my own

7. I trust in myself.

8. I draw strength from my inner light.

9. I am a unique gift to the world.

10. I may be one in billions, but I'm also one in a billion.

11. I matter, and the things I have to give matter.

12. I am a bright a star and offer as much as anyone else to the world.

13. I believe in my intuition and inner wisdom.

14. I forgive myself for my mistakes.

15. I let go of anger so that I may see more clearly.

16. I take responsibility for the ways my anger has hurt others.

17. Every situation happens for a reason

18. I will breath in calm and breathe out my nervous energy.

19. I deserve wonderful things to happen in my life.

20. I replace anger with compassion and understanding.

21. I apologize to those I've hurt in the past with my negativity.

22. There is good to be found in every situation. Even if I cannot see it.

23. I choose to view things in optimistic and hopeful ways.

24. I will ask for guidance and help if I cannot see the way myself.

25. I will not give up because there are still things to try and do.

26. I have a power and courage that rests deep inside me.

27. I love all of my family, even if they don't understand who I am.

28. I will let my wisdom guide me into making the right decision.

29. I will take in all feedback, but I will use my own judgment to make a final decision.

30. I will move past my inner conflict and find the peace that is around it.

31. My family is a gift not a burden.

32. I am the person I am today because of the lessons my family has taught me.

33. I will show and tell the people around me that I love and value them.

34. I choose friends who will love me and approve of me.

35. I will only surround myself with those who lift me up and not tear me down.

36. I am smart and beautiful. The people around me see me the same way.

37. I will take my pleasure from my friends and there success, even if we sometime disagree or have different views on an issue.

38. I have the strength to leave a situation if it is not good for me.

39. Every new person I meet opens up a world of possibilities.

40. New people teach me more about my own life every day.

41. I am pursuing the things I find both fulfilling and enjoyable.

42. I pursue both rewarding and meaningful work.

43. I play a major role in my own success.

44. I believe in the ability I have and what it can do for others.

45. I let go of all the negative thoughts that are in my head.

46. This day will bring me joy and happiness.

47. My thoughts become my reality so I'll have only positive thoughts.

48. Today will be a day to remember for all the right reasons.

49. I will participate fully in my own life.

50. I let go of any worries that will drain all of my energy.

51. I trust in my abilities to provide for those around me.

52. I am the decision maker of my future.

53. I will attract wealth and fortune in abundance.

54. Money will come to me like a magnet.

55. I will find success in whatever path I take.

56. I make bold, calculated and well informed plans for the future.

57. I show patience in helping my family understand all of my dreams.

58. I will ask my family to support me in all my endeavors.

59. I will answer questions about my goals and dreams without letting it make me defensive.

60. I will continue down the path of my choosing no matter what the obstacle in front of me.

61. My loved one will love me even when they don't completely understand me.

62. I will accept everyone that is around me for who and what they are.

63. I cannot change others, I can only change myself.

64. I am safe and all is well.

65. Everything will work out in my favor.

66. I have the strength to get through any situation.

67. Every problem has its own solution.

68. I will attempt all – not only some – ways to find a solution to my problems.

69. The answer is in front of me. All I have to do is see it.

70. I will look at a problem from all angles.

71. I have no right to be compared, or compare, myself to anyone. No one can know a person's full story.

72. I choose to see the light I have to offer the world around me.

73. I will work on myself a little each day and be a better person for it.

74. I am happy living in my own skin and with my current set of circumstances.

75. Giving up is an option for another day.

76. It will always be too early for me to give up on my goals.

77. I believe in my path so I will continue to press on.

78. The past won't hold any power over me from this point on.

79. All I need is given to me at the proper time and place.

80. Happiness is my given birthright.

81. I will share my joy and humor with those around me.

82. I admire and respect my partner. I value them as they value me.

83. I will communicate both my needs and desires clearly.

84. I am successful today. I'll be successful tomorrow. I'll always be successful.

85. I will take bold action in spite of any fear I may feel.

86. I will constantly challenge myself with new opportunities.

87. I will take the time to listen to those around me and get to know them.

88. I'm deeply fulfilled knowing the person that I've become.

89. I live fully in the present. I will not take my life at this moment for granted.

90. I embrace change and will adapt to any new situation.

91. I am healthy, well groomed, and brimming with confidence.

92. I attract only the best circumstances and the best people.

93. I have integrity and I am a person of my word.

94. I will sow the seeds of peace no what where I am at.

95. I am grateful for every moment I am given.

96. I will observe all my thoughts and actions without being judgmental.

97. Staying relaxed and calm energizes my entire being.

98. All of my muscles are relaxing, and all of the tension in my body is being released.

99. I transcend stress and live with my inner peace.

100. Every day I become more at ease with who I am, and who I'm trying to become.

101. All is well. I'm am content, happy and fulfilled.

Conclusion

Thanks again for purchasing my book. I hope you have found the lessons inside as powerful as I did when first starting out. In order to achieve a new mindset you need to want to change. Negative thinking and skepticism will only hinder your ability to grow and embrace what I discussed during the course of this book.

When I was first starting out I was very resistant to change. I learned all about the power of mindset, and while I thought it was interesting, I wasn't ready to actually do the work and make a change. It took almost another year, and another set of difficult circumstances, until I was truly ready to do the work and make a change in my life. It was the best thing I ever did for myself.

While results didn't happen overnight I applied many of the ideas found in this book to my own life, and now a few years later my world has completely changed. I'm happier, and I've been more successful in both love and business. Having a successful mindset was a game changer in my life. If it worked for me, there's no reason it can't work for you!

Good luck on your journey of personal growth! I know you can do it!

Manufactured by Amazon.ca
Bolton, ON

24732854R00028